TREEHOUSES

PEAR TREE/JOHN HARRIS

THE HOUSE THAT JACK BUILT

TREEHOUSES

DAVID PEARSON

GAIA BOOKS LIMITED

A GAIA ORIGINAL

Books from Gaia celebrate the vision of Gaia, the self-sustaining living Earth, and seek to help its readers live in greater personal and planetary harmony.

Original concept for 'The House that Jack Built' series: Joss Pearson
Project Editor and Research: Helena Petre
Copy Editor: Christine Davis
Designer: Sara Mathews
Managing Editor: Pip Morgan
Production: Lyn Kirby
Direction: Patrick Nugent

First published in the United Kingdom in 2001 by Gaia Books Ltd,
   66 Charlotte Street, London W1T 4QE
and 20 High Street, Stroud, Gloucestershire GL5 1AZ
Visit our website: www.gaiabooks.co.uk with on-line book shop

ISBN 1 85675 137 6

A catalogue record of this book is available from the British Library.

Printed and bound by Oriental Press, Dubai.

10 9 8 7 6 5 4 3 2 1

Cover image and page 2: treehouses by Pear Tree, Scotland

"To Pier who loved his first treehouse"

CONTENTS

8
INTRODUCTION

14
BAMBOO HOOCH

18
TREESNAKES

22
THE ELMS

24
MARIAH'S MANOR

28
CANYON PERCH

30
THE OXBOW ANNEX

32
GREEN MAGIC NATURE RESORT

36
MISO BARREL TREEHOUSE

40
JUNGLE TREEHOUSE

44
THE ENGEL TREEHOUSE

48
OUT 'N' ABOUT RESORT

50
SAMSTREEHOUSE

54
THE TENTYRIS COMMUNITY

56
FAIRMILE PROTEST CAMP

58
THE SCURLOCK HOUSE

62
THREE-IN-ONE TREEHOUSE

64
THE GEODESIC DOME

66
BOOMERANG FARM

68
WOODPECKER HOTEL

70
THE BIOSPHERE TREE

74
PEAR TREE

78
CORBIN'S TREEHOUSE

80
MAKE IT

92
RESOURCES

94
INDEX

95
ACKNOWLEDGMENTS

ARBOREAL DELIGHTS

A TREEHOUSE.
A TREEHOUSE.
A SECRET YOU AND ME HOUSE.
A HIGH UP IN THE LEAFY BRANCHES HOUSE.
A HAPPY AS YOU CAN BE HOUSE.
A STREET HOUSE.
A NEAT HOUSE.
A BE SURE TO WIPE YOUR FEET HOUSE,
IS NOT THE KIND OF HOUSE FOR ME.
LET'S GO AND LIVE IN A TREEHOUSE.

(Anon.)

"I still get a shiver of excitement when I recall my part in the joyful creation of this delightful and spirited little treehouse," says designer and builder David Kibbey (see The Engel Treehouse, p. 44). Treehouses do indeed evoke deep, sometimes strange, emotions. They may remind us of happy childhood days spent building dens and hideaways, or they may arouse primal instincts inherited from our ancestors' arboreal times as tree-dwellers. Whatever the subconscious drives, there is no doubt that being in a treehouse is a beautiful and intimate experience. Perched up in the leafy canopy of a tree with the clouds and sky above, surrounded by wildlife and the natural world, you cannot help but feel in harmony with yourself and with nature. The gentle swaying of the tree, much like a boat on a lake, calms and transports you far away from the cares of the earthbound world. The story of treehouses leads to a magical world of fun and fantasy, where imaginations can run free.

Mention a treehouse and the first image that will spring to mind will probably be from a children's story. It might be the castaway Swiss Family Robinson and their beloved shipwreck treehouse, or the ingenious jungle treehouse belonging to Tarzan — especially as depicted in old Hollywood movies. You might think of the comfortable hollow-tree houses of Winnie-the-Pooh's friends Owl and Christopher Robin, or the magical elven city of the Galadhrim in J.R.R. Tolkien's *Lord of the Rings* — where, high up in the Mallorn trees, the Hobbits come upon a talan, a high platform as big as the deck of a ship. For others it might be a memorable visit to Disneyland in Anaheim, California, and the ascent through the trees to the Swiss Family Robinson treehouse — even if it is built of plastic and concrete when you get there.

Treehouses have a remarkable history, and have long been used by the indigenous peoples of the South Pacific and South-east Asia. The Kombai and Korowai peoples of West Papua and Papua New Guinea traditionally lived in treehouses "like nests of giant birds", according to one visitor; built 100 ft (30 metres) above the ground, these were places of safety and security from wild animals, mosquitoes and marauding tribes. In the 1700s, the English navigator Captain Cook recorded an encounter with treetop dwellers in Tasmania.

In the Western world, meanwhile, treehouses were leisure fantasies. The Roman emperor Caligula held sumptuous banquets in a giant plane tree; during the Italian Renaissance members of the Medici family vied with each other to create the most magnificent marble treehouse; and in Tudor England there was mention of "roosting places", while Queen

MARY EVANS PICTURE LIBRARY

EXOTIC APPEAL: AN ILLUSTRATION C.1850 SHOWS A TIBETAN LAMA MEDITATING IN A TREEHOUSE.

Elizabeth I herself dined in a massive linden tree. In the mid-eighteenth century a small half-timbered treehouse was built at Pitchford Hall, near Shrewsbury, England. Queen Victoria visited as a thirteen-year-old princess in 1832, recording in her journal that "I went up a staircase to a little house in a tree". It still survives, and is one of the oldest treehouses in existence.

Also surviving today is a remarkable French 'tree church' at Allouville-Bellefosse, Normandy. In Paris in the 1900s, Parc Robinson was a popular restaurant rendezvous boasting a *point de vue magnifique* from the trees. The American novelist Mary Austin, meanwhile, wrote her books in the open-air writing room of her "wick-i-up" at Carmel, California. In 1952 at one of the most famous treehouses, Treetops in Kenya, Queen Elizabeth II ascended as a princess and descended as a queen after taking the oath of accession to the throne following the death of her father, George VI. Another remarkable story is that of Bob Redman who, in the 1980s, managed to build a dozen or so treehouses in New York's Central Park before being discovered by the authorities.

A new dimension to treehouses is their use as quickly erected structures to house activists protesting against tree felling and road building.

A renowned example is the 'treesit' by Julia Butterfly Hill high up in a California redwood, begun in 1997. In the UK, many protest treehouses have come and gone since the first at Jesmond Dene, Newcastle, in 1993.

Treehouses today are undergoing a renaissance. Much credit for this must go to pioneers such as Peter Nelson ('Mr Treehouse' to his friends), co-founder of Treehouse Workshop, who has inspired many to take up treehouse building and given enough practical building advice to get anyone started. As well as there being increasing numbers of individuals building their own structures, there now exist a number of specialist professional companies – Treehouse Workshop and John Harris's Pear Tree company in Scotland among them – who will undertake the whole process from design to construction. There is even a World Treehouse Association, a network for treehouse dreamers, builders and livers who get together and share experiences at their annual conferences at Michael Garnier's Out 'n' About Resort in Oregon, USA.

If you want to sample treehouse living before building your own there are numerous bed-and-breakfast treehouses for rent around the world. These are often in stunning locations

DARIO NOVELLINO/STILL PICTURES

TRADITIONAL WAY OF LIFE: HANUNOO-MANGYAN TREEHOUSE ON MINDORO ISLAND, THE PHILIPPINES.

and may be either remote single treehouses or part of a "tree hotel" or "eco-lodge" in a leisure resort or protected wilderness area. Start looking on the Web and you will find plenty of possibilities (see Resources).

So what are treehouses used for? Well, just about anything and everything: kids' playhouses; adult refuges and retreats; places for peaceful study and meditation; unusual locations for social gatherings, whether cocktail parties or wedding receptions; offices; permanent homes; and wildlife hides or observatories. A treehouse can be just a simple deck with a rope ladder, or an ambitious two- or three-storey structure with all facilities including a living area, bedrooms, a bathroom and a kitchen. There are now increasing numbers of eco-friendly treehouses, which use only salvaged materials and equipment; water is collected and recycled, photovoltaic panels provide electricity, and double-glazed windows make for a comfortable and energy-conserving interior.

Treehouses can last for many years, and often pass through various phases. One might begin as a weekend project for a children's playhouse; then the children themselves will make their own changes as they grow up, gradually transforming a play area into a party and study space. And when the children leave home the treehouse often starts a new lease of life: it might become anything from guestroom to retreat, storeroom or office – with different functions coming and going over time. If nothing else, a treehouse is certainly versatile.

J. BENECKI

THE 'SECRET TREEHOUSE': A TWO-STOREY HIDEAWAY BUILT INTO AN OLD MAPLE AND LIVED IN ALL YEAR.

The extraordinary stories in this book will give a taste of the diversity of motifs for building treehouses, and the range of individual responses to the treehouse urge. Every treehouse is different, and each owner/dweller has his or her own tale to tell. It is also fascinating to see how the simple desire to build a treehouse has affected so many people's lives, and has led to some quite unexpected outcomes.

Sam Edwards built his highly eccentric structure almost entirely from salvaged items (see p. 50): it boasts an airplane bedroom and a bathroom housed in a submarine-shaped prop originally built for an Elvis Presley movie. For Lesley Gillilan, a visitor to the Green Magic Nature Resort — an eco-friendly treehouse among the hills of Kerala in southern India (see p. 32) — even the exotic wildlife "couldn't quite compete with the first jaw-dropping sight of our treehouse accommodation: a palm-thatched timber lodge, cradled in the upper branches of a giant ficus tree, 90 ft off the ground". If you are thinking of living in recycled miso barrels, then John-san (see p. 36) will tell you about how he did this in Japan. Not only did he build a beautiful treehouse but he was also inspired to start Treehab, a tree climbing group for people with physical disabilities or learning difficulties. His stated aim is to bring people and trees together, for the benefit of both the trees and the community as a whole.

As John-san would no doubt agree, treehouses are nothing without the trees themselves. Direct action to save threatened trees and natural habitats has grabbed the headlines in recent years, and Simon tells us what it was like to be part of a tree protest camp in the UK (see p. 56). Radicalism can take many forms: artist Mikael Genberg wanted to create a series of alternative dwelling-places for people to experience, and his Woodpecker Hotel treehouse in Västerås, Sweden (see p. 68) has now accommodated more than 250 guests. Add to these Australian treehouses at Boomerang Farm and in the Blue Mountains; the Bamboo Hooch in Puerto Rico; the Biosphere Tree in Hawaii, and more — and you can see that treehouses are truly a global phenomenon.

So why not partake of these arboreal delights? Read, and be inspired by, the fascinating stories of the treehouse builders and dwellers featured in this book. Use the Make It section to pick up some basic tips and practical advice. Look at the Resources listings for further information and contacts. Then get started on building your own treehouse without delay.

PUTTING DOWN ROOTS

Jo Scheer: We sailed to Puerto Rico after years of Caribbean adventure — me, Laura, our five-year-old son Sam, and a daughter on the way, to be named Sophia. Living on board our boat *Bamboo*, we had worked and played on St John — where Laura had a landscaping business and I did my bamboo work, making everything from lamps to store interiors — and had eventually sailed the lesser Antilles and the north coast of South America.

It was a carefree time that I will always treasure. But our love of plants was somewhat hindered by the onboard lifestyle — and, with our new family, we needed room to grow. So it was time to finally realize our need of land, and end our life on the water.

After some false starts we settled in Rincon, a small surfing town on Puerto Rico's western tip. Here we found the land, the soil, the rain and the sunsets. But the search for a house, a task involving daily bicycle treks throughout the peninsula, proved disappointing. Eventually we realized that we would have to build — but where?

As I coasted down a hill one day I noticed an overgrown path, closed off long ago. I worked my way through the barbed wire and followed the path to a grove of ancient mango trees, two giant genip trees, and a ruined foundation in the middle. The porch stood in almost perfect repose, its molded concrete flowerpots peeking through the overgrown foliage. This is it, I thought — it was so magical, so heavy with a sense of place.

I discovered that the property was indeed for sale. When we took over the 12 acre (5 ha) plot in 1992 it was in dire need of attention. Over the next

JO SCHEER

"THE FINAL DESIGN WAS DICTATED BY THE SITE AND THE MATERIALS." A HIP ROOF PROTECTS AGAINST HURRICANES – THE FAMILY HAVE TO DATE SURVIVED THREE, WITH MINIMAL DAMAGE.

seven years, while raising our new family, we built our tropical treehouse, landscaped the land, and sold our boat. It has been a labor of love, the culmination of all our daydreams, and a fine place to grow up, for all of us.

Our treehouse came to be known as the 'hooch'. It is located off our outside bathroom, and accessed via a short bridge. I built it myself over a period of several months. The process was relatively simple: I collected the raw materials (bamboo poles toppled by a hurricane), designed the structure, prefabricated most of the roof and then assembled it on site.

The bamboo poles were over 23 ft (7 m) long and of a species native to Colombia, *Guadua angustifolia*. Not only is this species rot- and termite-resistant but it's also strong, and does not split. All the same, I made sure all the joinery was through-bolted with treated wood inserts for strength.

The final design was dictated by both the site and the characteristics of the materials. Outward-leaning poles allow the foundation of the treehouse to be minimized, while the upper attachment (the bridge) is used for stability. The wide overhang allows minimum direct sun and rain on the bamboo, thus maximizing its durability. The floor is 10 x 14 ft (3 x 4.3 m) and the roof is proportionally much larger, of a hip type that slopes on all four sides, with a central skylight.

Hurricane resistance was an important consideration. The hip roof helps this (because it always has a sloping side facing the wind) as does the minimal wall area. The south-facing roof area incorporates two 12-volt photovoltaic collectors, providing power for the fan over the double bed, a reading light, and landscape lighting.

We are currently taking a sabbatical in the cold north, and so the hooch serves as the master bedroom for our vacation rental. We will return, but for now our tropical home is available for like-minded people to enjoy.

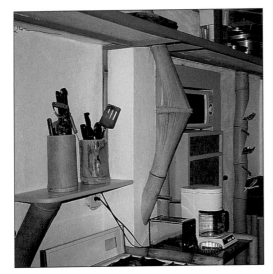

JO SCHEER

"BAMBOO", SAYS JO SCHEER, "IS ONE OF THE MOST VERSATILE – AND DURABLE – MATERIALS THERE IS."
HE HAS USED IT THROUGHOUT HIS FAMILY'S TROPICAL HOME.

WOODLAND WAYS

Hazel and Filbert: Back in 1989, we purchased 10 acres (4 ha) of woodland in North Central Minnesota. The land had not been developed, so it was without a road or modern utilities. We spent the first few years just getting to know the lay of the land – such as how the river fluctuates from season to season – and discovering the ins and outs of woodland recreation.

Finally, in 1995, we began to think seriously about putting up a structure on the river so that we could stay there overnight in relative comfort. (Being in our fifties now, we are no longer inclined to sleep on the ground.) But first we had to put in a trail. This took one entire summer of work, after which we were ready to begin hauling materials to the river.

The following spring we selected the site for our treehouse. The idea of a treehouse seemed to come naturally. We weren't ready to build a permanent structure, and yet we wanted something very close to the river. Putting a small structure in the trees seemed the most eco-friendly and sensible solution. It became known as our 'Treesnakes' project.

The site we chose had a group of maples and oaks perfectly spaced for a room of 8 x 10 ft (2.5 x 3 m) with a small 'bridge' from the top of the hill for the dogs to gain access as well.

The materials we chose were all purchased at the local lumber superstore. We didn't want a lot of weight on the trees, so we picked lightweight products: we thus have tongue-in-groove pine siding and a metal roof lined with styrofoam sheeting. The floor is of simple green treated lumber covered with thin painted plywood. The

HAZEL AND FILBERT

BACK TO NATURE: HAZEL AND FILBERT SPENT YEARS GETTING TO KNOW
THE WOODLAND BEFORE CHOOSING A SITE FOR THEIR TREEHOUSE.

single-paned windows are aluminum-framed, of a type usually installed outside ordinary windows for added insulation from the cold. Later, we added a small propane gas heater with an automatic turn-off in case of oxygen depletion in the cabin.

Just last year the 5 acres (2 ha) adjoining us to the south became available. We were very excited to be able to purchase this lot and add it to our existing 10 acres. Now we could start work on building the road. Having acquired higher ground on the south, we were able to avoid the low, swampy areas in the middle of our property. We cut the rough road in fall 1999 – so long to the old, rocky trail!

With the treehouse being so small, it became obvious that we needed a shed both for storage and for bunking the dogs down at night. Filbert used exterior siding for the walls, and transparent plastic roofing for light. During the winter, of course, the dogs sleep in the treehouse with us.

The best advice we can give to anyone inspired to build a structure in the trees is to first find the right trees. The house will succeed only if it has a proper framework. When you've chosen the trees, graph them out on paper and decide on the platform dimensions. Once the platform is secure, the rest is just building walls, windows, doors, and so on.

We'd also recommend keeping the materials as light as possible, and consulting all the treehouse sources you can find – both at the library and on the internet. Don't expect to have all the details, but look carefully at the photos on these websites, and consult standard construction guides for building techniques. The best purchase we made was a cordless saw and drill set. No need for noisy generators!

Since there are just the two of us, we used our common sense and a good deal of patience. It took us two years to complete the treehouse – from constructing the platform in fall

1997 to our first overnight with the new radiant heater in the fall of 1999. We still have work to complete, such as the exterior raised platform that we intend to use for star-gazing at night.

The best thing about having our treehouse is knowing that we can go to sleep to the sound of the leaves swirling overhead with the wind. At night we look out of the windows at the stars over the river and know that we are free from the confines of earth. It's a little like hanging in a hammock: even if you're not actually moving, you're still 'suspended'. In spring the river comes right up and under our treehouse. Fog hangs over the river on early summer mornings. The deep croaking of the night frogs have a rhythm all their own.

We've become confident now, and have decided to build a permanent home up here on the river within five years. This will be our retirement place when we leave the city for good. We hope that the little treehouse will stand in the big maples and oaks for a long, long time, and bring magic to all who stay in her.

HAZEL AND FILBERT

"A TREEHOUSE MEANT THAT WE COULD STAY OVERNIGHT BY THE RIVER IN RELATIVE COMFORT."

PIONEER SPIRIT

Val Oliver: I have no treehouse to call my own, yet in some way the treehouse at The Elms has become woven into my family history. Every year we hold a family reunion in Australia's Blue Mountains, New South Wales. With at least fifteen adults and five young children that means renting a couple of houses – one of which is an old timber homestead called The Elms. And one of the best things about it – for the children especially – is the old treehouse that stands in the grounds.

To approach The Elms you pass through a grove of mature pine trees on the edge of an escarpment. From there the views across the Blue Mountains, over gorges and towards distant outcrops, are magnificent. The smell of eucalyptus and pine needles drifts all around, and overhead you can hear the call of the kurrawongs – a marvellous, penetrating warble.

The treehouse, when you reach it, is essentially very simple: rough and rustic, echoing the the main house, which was built in the 1880s by the present owner's great-grandfather. The Elms is very much in the traditional style of the early white settlers: timber weatherboard construction with a corrugated iron roof, and corrugated iron bullnose verandahs on three sides. The treehouse is made from what looks like offcuts from the roof iron, or recycled bits from house repairs. The staircase seems to be made of thinnings from the property's many trees. One thing is certain: the children all make a beeline for it whenever they come over.

We could not go to The Elms last year, as the main house was being refurbished and renovated. I do hope the character has been preserved, as its early pioneering history clung around it in its pre-renovation state.

VAL OLIVER

ROUGH AND RUSTIC, THE ELMS TREEHOUSE ECHOES THE SPIRIT OF THE MAIN RESIDENCE.
FOR SEVEN-YEAR-OLD CRAIG, IT'S AN ADVENTURE PLAYGROUND.

SAVING THE REDWOODS

Nate Madsen: I began my occupation of this one-thousand-year-old redwood, Mariah, in 1998. One day on my way home from work I realized that I just couldn't watch another great tree go, so up I climbed. At first my home consisted of just branches: I spent the first three nights resting directly in Mariah's arms. Construction began on day four, as I realized that if I was going to stay, and keep Mariah safe from harm, it was going to require more than just a small nest. Mariah's Manor has been an ongoing project ever since then.

I did all the construction work myself, employing reused builders' leftovers or sustainably harvested lumber provided by a friend of mine who is a responsible private logger. The home has three tiers, and construction progressed from top to bottom.

The top deck is made from sustainably harvested wood. It rests 170 ft (52 m) above the ground and has an incredible view towards the ocean to the west and beautiful ridge lines to the far south, east and north; in between is a checkerboard landscape of vast forests and clearings. Initially the deck measured 3 × 5 ft (9 × 1.5 m) but it has now grown into an elbow shape that wraps around two sides of the tree. This provides a sun deck and a place to tend my little garden.

Below this is a platform of 3 × 7 ft (0.9 × 2.1 m); this is where I spent my first winter. It is tarped in and proved moderately dry, but I did get soaked from time to time and so for the following winter I built what is now the living space. The mid-level platform is now used to house electrical equipment and my solar power system,

NATE MADSEN

HORRIFIED BY THE ONGOING DESTRUCTION OF CALIFORNIA'S ANCIENT REDWOODS,
NATE MADSEN MADE 'MARIAH' HIS TREETOP HOME.

which was donated to me by Alternative Energy Engineering in Redway, California. It uses hand-me-down solar panels from Julia Butterfly Hill, another tree protestor in California. With this system I'm able to supply all my own power to my laptop computer, which I used to finalize the details of my BSc in physical science from Humboldt State University. I also charge all my own phone and video camera batteries, flashlight, blender for smoothies, and so on, and usually have power to spare.

At 125 ft (38 m) rests the bulk of the project and living space. This was built in the fall of 1999 after a winter of heavy rains and snowstorms, and took most of the summer to plan. It was very difficult to figure out how to begin as there was no place to set supplies or tools, and no foundation to start with. Once things got rolling, however, it became easier.

Nearly all the materials for this level are recycled, although I did use new anchor rope to ensure a strong and reliable support system. The roof and walls are of reused fiberglass (salvaged during a demolition job I had some years back) and reused plastic from the brewery where I used to work.

The dimensions of this level are 5 × 10 ft (1.5 × 3 m). Despite the fact that it has branches growing through the floor and walls, there is minimal leakage – although in pounding rain, when there are winds above 65 mi (100 km) an hour, I do get a few drips from the branches. Attached to this main level is an open entrance measuring 4 × 4 ft (1.2 × 1.2 m); this serves as a place to greet guests, and an area to bath and do daily duties.

Mariah's Manor has a water collection system that delivers rainwater from the 'roof' to an internal storage tank. This holds about 18 US gallons (70 litres) when full, and it supplies all my water needs for about nine months of the year. There is an overflow hose that delivers the extra water back into the natural hydrologic cycle; when a dry spell is approaching this can be used to fill alternative storage, thus boosting capacity to around 40 US gallons (150 litres).

During the other three months of the year I rely on kind neighbors who deliver me what I need to survive. They are the lifeblood of this action, and are responsible for the life of this tree and for my survival.

To cook I use one of two methods, depending on my feeling at that moment and what fuel supply is on hand. I waver between cooking on a small gas burner and on a 'rocket stove' that can boil a pot of water with one small stick. The first has the drawback of using gas, but the rocket stove pollutes the air more notably with its smoke. I think the real solution to this dilemma is to eat raw foods, but my love of hot tea and passion for good hot food drives me to compromise. Maybe one day I'll give up the cooking, maybe not. We all draw the line as best we can, given where we are at any given time. In general, I try to make myself as cosy as possible, as life is a gift to be treasured and shared.

NATE MADSEN

NATE USES SOLAR PANELS TO WORK ON HIS DEGREE AND GRADUATES IN UNUSUAL FASHION.

OUTDOOR ROOM WITH A VIEW

Barbara Butler: I've been making play spaces for children for thirteen years. I love creating 'outdoor rooms' that are the kids' special getaway – places where they can dream, read, have friends to visit, race around, climb all over, or simply stay out in nature. Each structure is special, with secret hiding places, escape doors, carvings and climbing opportunities – a combination of physical and imaginative play. I strive to create a special spot in the yard that's strong, safe, magical and distinctly different from the adult world, especially since kids today can't roam around as freely as I did as a child.

A treehouse is perhaps the most perfect playhouse. I love attaching structures to the trees when I can, or at least putting them in the trees' canopy. Canyon Perch was created for a couple in Marin County, California, whose two grandchildren live nearby. Finding that they had to cut down a large tree, the grandparents decided that instead of taking it right to the ground they would cut the tree off at 9 ft (3 m) and ask me whether I could do anything with it. Was I excited!

The property is set at the top of a ravine with an incredible view of Mount Tamalpais, and I wanted to make the most of the spectacular site. I came up with the idea of a swinging bridge leading to a deck on top of the stump, with a playhouse in the middle. From the deck you can slide down a fireman's pole or go through the trapdoor and take the ladder to the bridge below. Down below is another play room with a secret escape.

Like all my work it's painted in custom hues and constructed of solid redwood. I see my structures as works of art that will last for decades – to be enjoyed by children and adults alike.

TEENA ALBERT

"A TREEHOUSE IS THE MOST PERFECT PLAYHOUSE – AND THIS WAS A PERFECT SPOT."
THE BRIGHTLY PAINTED PLAY SPACE OVERLOOKS A DRAMATIC RAVINE.

BUILDING THE DREAM

Karen Grayczk: It all started with two maple trees growing at our home in Oregon. I had a dream of building a treehouse in their branches, but heavy fall winds left us with a two-ton branch in the yard and sinking hearts. We called an arborist to cut away the dead wood and install supportive cabling between the branches. Fortunately he pronounced the trees healthy enough, so we began buying lumber and I managed to salvage some pressure-treated poles from a nearby hop farm.

We made the foundation out of poles, then put up the basic platform – allowing plenty of room for the tree to carry on growing – and started laying decking boards. A broken branch in one of the maples was cut off to support the second level. We built walls in the trees – the first was so heavy it had to be supported on one side by a fallen tree that we cut to size.

Slowly but surely the treehouse grew – here a wall, there a can of beer, until platform number two was in place and we could start building a loft and putting up rafters for the roof. We bought some windows and a Dutch door from salvage and adapted the final design around them, adding a green metal roof. We also installed a railing around the upper deck, and now plan to do the same for the stairs. I'm currently having fun working on the interior, which is to be a riot of jungle-meets-East India décor.

The treehouse was named after the original structure we had as children, built by my father and brothers. We lived then in a very wooded area close to Oxbow Park, and after we moved away we referred to that home as 'Oxbow'. We called the new treehouse 'Oxbow Annex' in memory of my father, who passed away two years ago.

KAREN GRAYCZK

A BROKEN BRANCH AND A FALLEN TREE WERE PUT TO GOOD USE IN THE
OXBOW ANNEX, A HOMAGE TO CHILDHOOD TREEHOUSE MEMORIES.

PALM-THATCHED PENTHOUSE

Lesley Gillilan: We were sharing a pot of afternoon tea on the terrace of the Green Magic Nature Resort in south India's Wyanad Hills, when my companion (photographer Dave Young) spotted a Giant Malabar squirrel flying through the upper branches of the nearby trees. I grabbed my binoculars and just caught a glimpse of the creature's yellow face, its oversized paws and the rich red fur of its tail before it disappeared into the rainforest.

Earlier that day we had watched a family of Bonnet monkeys perform acrobatics in the branches of the same trees and, later, a walk through the tropical forest had been rewarded by glimpses of lion-tailed macaques, numerous varieties of birds and butterflies, and even a scary close encounter with a wild elephant.

The natural environment was what had inspired us to make the long, arduous journey into northern Kerala's mountain rainforests, but even the rarest and most exotic species of wildlife couldn't quite compete with the first jaw-dropping sight of our treehouse accommodation: a palm-thatched timber lodge, cradled in the upper branches of a giant ficus tree, 90 ft (27 m) off the ground.

Guests are transported to their treetop room by an indigenous cane elevator, a simple bentwood cage supported on ropes and pulleys and crudely, but effectively, counterbalanced by a pail of water. I had to be cajoled into it, but the views from the top were worth every vertiginous inch of the agonizing journey upward. From a bedroom, which was furnished with traditional Keralan materials and featured an en suite bathroom (with flushing toilet and shower) and an al fresco verandah, we looked down on the resort

DAVE YOUNG

WHAT COULD BE MORE ROMANTIC THAN A NIGHT HIGH ABOVE THE RAINFOREST
– WITH AN ECO-FRIENDLY POWER SUPPLY, OF COURSE.

through a paradise of tropical flora. Creature comforts are a little primitive (the water is ice cold), but a handy pair of binoculars is provided and there is room service of sorts – you can lean over the verandah, make a rough impersonation of a cuckoo, and a tray of tea is duly winched up in the lift.

The rustic tree-hut look of the place belies the intelligent thinking behind its creation. An experiment in low-impact eco-tourism, the resort was devised by Keralan tour operator Babu Varghese, who was a zoologist before setting up his travel company, Tourindia, in the 1970s. Green Magic utilizes 500 acres (200 ha) of redundant cardamom plantation in a conservation area and provides employment for the landless tribal people who once worked the plantation. For the visitor, it presents an opportunity to enjoy what remains of India's southern rainforests (thousands of acres were destroyed by colonial tea planters) without harming the delicate balance of nature.

Eco-friendly, explains Babu, means no generators, hence the treehouses are romantically lit with kerosene lamps. Solar panels provide auxiliary lighting and the resort's six bullocks create enough dung to provide traditional Indian 'bio-gas' for cooking. The food is home-grown and organic, and the two treehouses not only blend beautifully with the environment but also, says Babu, provide a safe haven away from mosquitos, predators and the occasional Indian tiger.

Animals, however, do occasionally intrude. On our first day, there were problems with the water because an elephant had stamped on the supply pipe. On our second we slept uneasily under the glare of a full moon, to the hooting of owls and the rustle of falling ficus leaves, and woke to find our socks had been nibbled in the night by tiny forest rats. Babu made no apologies. They are part of the authentic jungle life after all and, as he points out, the animals were there first.

DAVE YOUNG

VERTIGO SUFFERERS NEED NOT APPLY: AN INDIGENOUS CANE ELEVATOR
IS THE ONLY WAY UP AT THE GREEN MAGIC NATURE RESORT.

GOING AGAINST THE GRAIN

John-san: Our family treehouse, built of old miso barrels, sits in the grounds of a Buddhist temple within the forests of a national park. We always wanted our treehouse to be distinctly Japanese; but even more important to me was that it should be made from recycled materials, and that its creation should involve a wide community of people. The fact that it exists at all is a great tribute to the scores of volunteers who helped to make it possible.

From the start, the project attracted a lot of attention. The very idea of a liveable, environmentally-friendly treehouse, built by a foreigner and on temple lands ... people thought I was crazy. But the dream has come true.

Part of our treehouse statement was about recycling wood, and that's where the barrels came in. The miso and soy sauce-making industry has been replacing its big wooden barrels with stainless steel ones, and because of their overpowering smell the old barrels have usually been burnt rather than recycled. We wanted to show that, with ingenuity and elbow grease, they could become a valuable building material. Indeed, my wife Hiroko and I realized that the barrels would be perfect for a treehouse, as each was just the right size for a circular room!

The first task was to get the barrels from the factory, hose them down thoroughly, and hoist them up; we then built a wooden platform deck which we supported with two hundred recycled telephone poles. (We always avoided using nails in the trees.) We then placed the barrels on the deck to form individual rooms. These were imaginatively designed by Hiroko, who must take all the credit for making the

JOHN GATHRIGHT

"SOME TREEHOUSES LOSE THEIR 'TREEHOUSE' FEEL WHEN YOU'RE INSIDE. I WOULD STRONGLY RECOMMEND HAVING A TREE GROWING UP THROUGH THE CENTRE."

treehouse a home — if it had just been me, it would have ended up like something Tarzan would have lived in.

The treehouse is roughly pentagonal in shape, and is supported on each corner by a different tree. Every side is a slightly different length, to accommodate the five supporting trees, and the house sways in strong winds. Growing through the centre is a tsubaki tree, which flowers bright red in winter; our children like to play in it and hang toys and paintings in its branches. In summer the space around the tree creates natural air conditioning: a sunlight-heated pipe in the roof draws cool air into the house from around the tree trunk.

The second floor has no walls. Through the skylight we can track the course of the moon, stars and seasons — and move our bed to follow them.

I find that trees and treehouses seem to bring out the best in people, and trees — that's one of the reasons why I founded a tree-climbing school. The school has now helped over 1,400 people enjoy the treetops. The initial inspiration came from a special friend, Mrs Hikosaka; I first spotted her from 80 ft (24 m) up in the treetops, as two assistants struggled to push her small, frail body in its wheelchair across the forest floor. When she reached my tree, with all her strength, she half-yelled, half-whispered, "I would give everything in the world to leave this wheelchair and sit in the treetops with you!" A year later Mrs Hikosaka and I were shedding tears of joy in the treetop. Inside that frail, mangled body was a strong and courageous woman who had learned to climb trees.

Helping children and families into the treetops has since led us to create Treehab, a programme to help those with physical and learning difficulties to climb trees. Mrs Hikosaka (now a climbing instructor herself) continues to spur us on to more challenges. Having recently climbed a giant sequoia, our next goal is to share this amazing experience with disabled climbers.

JOHN GATHRIGHT

USING MISO BARRELS WAS A RADICAL IDEA, BUT IT WORKED. "TO BE HONEST", SAYS JOHN-SAN, "I CANNOT IMAGINE LIVING IN A GROUNDHOUSE ANY MORE."

GOING WITH THE FLOW

David Greenberg: My tree story begins twenty-five years ago when I was at graduate school in LA, specializing in urban design. I enrolled on a new experimental seminar called Man-Environment Relations, and we met at midnight in Death Valley every Friday.

One week, we had to present on the theme of "the perfect environment". It was close to 4 a.m. when it got to my turn. I talked about the beauty of nature that I had experienced recently on Hawaii: a valley with what seemed like 20,000 shades of green on the island of Maui; twisting red rivers of molten lava, like kinetic sculpture, on the Big Island; and a treehouse that I'd been to in Kauai. As far as I was concerned, the greatest creative force was "the big beach in the sky"; as designers we should remember that Man is unlikely to outdo Mother Nature.

Decades passed, and on New Year's Day, 1996, I began to design a treehouse on my 20-acre (8-ha) property at the jungle's edge in Hana on Maui. I began the project with great relish. I walked up into a big old kukui nut tree with a sketchpad and tried to design it. Nothing happened. The next day I took many pictures from different angles, studied them – still nothing.

For weeks I tried, but it didn't help. Eventually I went up to the tree, and looked at it for two minutes. I was going to just do it! The tree was in command here. I found two friends to help me – Jay had a lot of tools, and Joel a machete.

In a pile of discarded wood we found a long 2 x 4 in. (50 x 100 mm) piece of timber; it just spanned the distance from one kukui tree to another. We placed it arbitrarily at a height of

ROGER WEBSTER

GREENBERG'S ATTEMPTS TO DESIGN HIS TREEHOUSE ON PAPER CAME
TO NOTHING – "IN THE END I KNEW I HAD TO JUST DO IT!"

10 ft (3 m), where it became the end joist for the main floor of the treehouse. What to do next? Joel was hacking his way through some guava trees – they grow in abundance here – and we decided to use one to make a footing, placing it on top of a lava rock for extra height. We now had a triangular floor plan measuring 15 ft (4.5 m) on each side. In an hour we had created a plan that fifty hours of design couldn't have foreseen. The work had begun.

I now wanted to find some bamboo – fortunately not a problem on this side of Maui. I assembled my materials: the bamboo, guava wood, and various bits and pieces from the local dump. I decided to 'sketch' the rest of the design in full scale using bamboo pieces, tying them together like scaffolding in China.

When the skeleton structure was up, I called a visionary acquaintance in LA to tell him of my success. I had been working like a madman, getting up at the crack of dawn and laboring until dark. My acquaintance had a woman lawyer friend, Link Schwartz, who loved treehouses. The next morning in the fax machine I found a poem from her.

Just what I needed, a poem about a treehouse! Suddenly the tree felt different. It was a beautiful living thing, something of joy, to be honored. The poem changed me: I now had a viewpoint, one that was feminine and spiritual. Each limb of the tree took on a new meaning, to be dealt with both esthetically and functionally.

I had thought to build a stairway to the third level; instead, the poem led me to use the branches of the tree as a spiral stairway. Originally I planned to enclose most of the sleeping area; now I wanted to have lots of windows so I could see and feel the tree around me, especially the knots in the limbs. I even created a space on the main floor that has to be reached by crawling under or over a major limb. The space took on a greater meaning through the timeless feel of the tree surrounding me.

Treehouse Me

I long to be aloft in a tree
The limbs of an elm gently cradling me.
To ponder, star-gaze, or perhaps just to dream
Of quests and journeys as yet unforeseen.
Realities shift and visions unfold
Of what can be and is yet untold.
Its name shall be Ashtabula's Arms,
Majestic and bold with infinite charms.
Color me there in spirit and soul
Until I attain my dream; this goal.

(Link Schwartz)

ROGER WEBSTER

A POEM FROM A FRIEND INSPIRED SOME RADICAL CHANGES TO THE TREEHOUSE DESIGN. "THE SPACE TOOK ON A GREATER MEANING THROUGH THE TIMELESS FEEL OF THE TREE SURROUNDING ME."

FAMILY MATTERS

David Kibbey: It was in 1984 that I was approached by a couple, Larry and Stephanie Engel, who wanted to build a treehouse for their children (Laura and Brian, then aged five and two respectively). Larry, an attorney, felt all thumbs when it came to carpentry. Stephanie is a dreamer, meditator, poet, songwriter and composer, who was inspired to create a spirited fantasy environment for their children. I agreed to design and build the treehouse, on condition that the whole family would participate in the process.

Next to their Californian home, a magnificent old oak tree – already host to chirping birds, chattering squirrels and teeming insect life – cried out for a treehouse. Together, we built a house of 100 sq. ft (9 sq. m) boasting electrical circuits, a custom-made ladder, a deck and a hand-built Dutch door.

The oak grows right up through the roof and out of one windows – I had to invent 'tree gaskets' as a way of sealing out the extremes of weather. The Engel children are grown up now, but the treehouse still stands strong.

Work began with the 'consultation phase' – which consisted of the children climbing the tree. After thinking hard about what they wanted, the kids had lots of ideas and definite preferences. They asked for the entrance to be on the east, with their favorite curved branch to be 'furniture' inside the house. They hoped that the ladder would retract, and that they would be able to climb the tree from deck to roof. Additionally, they wanted a flat roof to allow for possible future expansion to a second floor, where we planned a spiral slide and a fireman's pole from the upper level to the deck.

DAVID KIBBEY

JOINT VENTURE: THE WHOLE FAMILY WAS INVOLVED IN PLANNING THE ENGEL
TREEHOUSE, WHICH STILL SITS PROUDLY IN ITS OLD OAK TREE.

The design and placement evolved through a natural sequence of events. We built the deck first, then walked it, measured it, and thought about it until the exact place and shape for the house grew from our combined imaginations. Larry helped carry recycled Californian redwood timbers up the hill and into the tree. Stephanie was the inspiration behind the whole project. For my part, I was very careful to maintain the health of the tree and to keep our childlike exuberance and enthusiasm rooted in solid practicality.

We still have some videotape of Brian, then aged five, playing in the treehouse with his friend. As a toddler, he had called it his 'tee house'. His conversation with this young pal is fascinating, as he describes his 'spiky little invisible friends' who live in the bark of the tree in the middle of the house. The young boys whispered all the time, so as not to disturb them.

Back to the building process: the light fixtures, the electrical parts, the windows, the structural beams, the wood trim, much of the hardware, and other features were all salvaged from contractors' demolition debris and spare parts. The house itself was built of painted plywood over a frame of 2 x 4 in. (50 x 100 mm) beams; we also used batt insulation and composition roll roofing. Clear vinyl and rubber strapping formed the 'treehouse gaskets', needed where the branches or trunk penetrated the roof and window.

For the access stair/ladder we made handrails from recycled copper piping and fittings. The base structure is balanced in the bottom notch of the oak tree, and the extremities of the deck and the house are hung with adjustable cables from heavy branches above. To prevent the tree from being chafed we put rubber hosepipe over cables. Most importantly, we ensured that no nails or bolts would penetrate the actual wood of the tree.

After the deck and house were completed, I was concerned that there might be too much wind-sway since the weight of the house was held by the branches. I therefore added two long posts, resting on pier blocks on the ground beneath, to support the heavy end of the deck. The entire structure is adjustable with bolts, allowing for tree growth and settling.

We also built a secure railing and gate around the base of the ladder – with the homeowner being a lawyer, the last thing he wanted was possible liability for inadvertent injury to passers-by. We figured that children who were tall enough to reach the high gate latch would be old enough to be able to negotiate the ladder safely.

Through the years, the house has served as a play- and guesthouse, meditation room, retreat, rabbit's home, storehouse and fantasy space. I still get a shiver of excitement when I recall my part in leading the joyful creation of this delightful and spirited little treehouse, harmoniously nestled among the flora and fauna of a California hillside.

DAVID KIBBEY

THE BEAUTIFULLY DETAILED HOUSE IS MADE PRIMARILY OF PAINTED PLYWOOD. LARRY ENGEL (RIGHT) INITIALLY FELT HE WAS 'ALL THUMBS' WHEN IT CAME TO CARPENTRY.

TIME OUT IN THE TREEPLEX

T.A. Allan: Most little boys dream of building a magical treehouse and spending the rest of their lives in it. Eventually, of course, they outgrow the fantasy. But not Michael Garnier. For he's the man behind the Out 'n' About Treehouse Resort in rural Takilma Valley, Oregon, where I worked for a time as resort manager.

In 1990, his fledgling bed and breakfast business foundering, Garnier built a treehouse up among the branches of a trio of oak trees. Today Garnier's resort features eleven treehouses, hosting 'treemusketeers' from all over the world. Two years after putting up that first treehouse, the Peacock Perch, Garnier constructed the Swiss Family Complex, a duplex of sorts, with the children's unit connected to the adult unit by a swinging bridge. Since then he has added the Treeplex, comprising an

18 ft (5.5 m) tipi on the ground, a 9 ft (2.75 m) tipi (the 'Treepee') in the trees and, across a swinging bridge, the stockade-style Cavaltree Fort, as well as the Treeroom School-house Suite and the Gatreebo.

The Treeroom Suite sleeps six and, with its extensive deck, is the grandest treehouse of them all. The Gatreebo, meanwhile, sits high off the ground in a large Douglas fir — and getting there involves traversing 120 ft (36 m) of canopy walkway.

All the treehouses are built of local woods. Uprights and underpinnings, as well as ridge poles and rafters, are from Douglas firs thinned from the local forests then dragged through the woods, trucked home and hand-peeled with draw knives.

The wooden treehouses feature fir exteriors and, for the most part, cedar interior panelling. The Treepee is sewn from canvas, as is the tented portion of the Cavaltree Fort and the top half of the walls in the Gatreebo.

Because the treehouses don't have concrete foundations, county officials initially refused to grant them building permits – but Garnier put them up anyway. An eight-year series of court battles ensued until finally, in 1998, the planning department was convinced of their structural integrity.

Garnier has now developed his own special 'artificial limb' system of attaching structures to trees. In the low tourist season he travels the world, building and consulting on treehouse projects from Florida to China.

T.A. ALLAN

"MAKING A TREEHOUSE IS A RELATIVELY SIMPLE MATTER – THE CHALLENGE IS SETTING UP THE PLATFORM UPON WHICH TO BUILD" SAYS MICHAEL GARNIER.

SALVAGE HEAVEN

Sam Isaac Edwards: I started building treehouses when I was about five or six. I didn't read a book – I just built. What little money I could gather together I spent not on candy and pop, but on nails and other basic construction supplies.

Over the years, using a triple-tree triangulated design, I created dozens of multi-level structures. However, my permanent residence, 'Samstreehouse', wasn't planned at all. I'd moved back to Calhoun, Georgia, after some years out West, when an old friend asked me to start a restaurant with him. I agreed, but told him I'd need a place to write. "Go up in the woods behind the restaurant and build," he simply replied.

With little thought to the location (right in the middle of town, close to the courthouse), I chose a 150-year-old, 60 ft (18 m) pin oak, sunk eight wooden supports under its north limb, and built a 8 × 16 ft (2.5 × 5 m) box enveloping a single limb. Then I got really carried away! The result was a 600 sq. ft (56 sq. m) treehouse on three levels, with limbs in every room. I simply built around them, with no design in mind.

Construction had begun in 1991. I scrounged old materials from wherever I could find them – windows from the old train depot, rusted tin from barns, chalkboard panelling from a disused school, pine flooring from a former slave cabin.

Once it had grown to liveable proportions, I found myself with a house with no utilities. So I had to lobby the town's decision-makers to assist me. My treehouse seemed to bring smiles to troubled faces, however, and I was finally granted water and power. I told

SAM EDWARDS

"I HAVEN'T THE FOGGIEST IDEA WHY I DECIDED THE HOUSE NEEDED AN AIRPLANE. I WAS LOOKING AT IT ONE DAY AND WONDERING WHAT TO DO NEXT, WHEN THE IDEA JUST POPPED INTO MY MIND."

the city inspector that I regretted placing him in such a position, and that really the building was the "evolution of a mistake". Looking up at me, the inspector replied, "I don't think that could be put any better."

Soon afterwards, a local farmer was discovered growing marijuana on plywood 'beds' in an industrial building. When the 'wacky backy' had been removed by the police, I was offered the board 'beds'. Two weeks later I had managed to convert them into a library and sitting room attached to the south end.

Later on, as I was looking at the treehouse and just wondering what to do next, 'airplane' simply flew into my mind! The 30 ft (9 m) wreck came from an air salvage yard. At a cost of about $300, it's the only addition I had to pay real money for.

A few months after the plane had evolved into a bedroom, I found an abandoned ski boat behind a friend's warehouse. He offered it to me and,

not wanting to offend, I took it. After being cradled on top of four railroad cross-ties, attached to the 'marijuana room' and enclosed, it became a very pleasant summer bedroom.

In the of spring of 2000, the same friend and I were out together when I noticed a nautical craft sitting in front of a marine supplier. It looked like a shabby submarine with a collapsed conning tower. I discovered that it was a prop, built for a 1960s Elvis movie.

After sinking another four railroad cross-ties I attached the sub to the north end, perpendicular to the airplane, where it is being converted into a shower and bathroom. Each extension is situated at a slightly different elevation – none obstructs the view of the others. This, I like to think, lends balance to the imbalance.

I never use new materials when salvage is available. Every 'adopted child' of this treehouse brings its own biography. The result is a unique and quite amazing multi-storied structure.

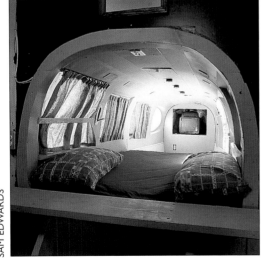

SAM EDWARDS

ENTIRE TREE LIMBS GROW INSIDE SAMSTREEHOUSE, WHICH ALSO FEATURES AN AIRLINE BEDROOM, A SKI BOAT 'EXTENSION' AND A ROOM MADE FROM FORMER MARIJUANA BEDS.

DO-IT-YOURSELF TREE-DEN

Lepre Viola: Founded in 1977, Damanhur is a federation of communities and a centre for spiritual research. Situated in the Valchiusella Valley in Piemonte, Italy, the federation has its own constitution, currency, schools and daily paper; there are over five hundred citizens. Tentyris is one of the five communities in the valley.

The Tentyris community treehouse was built in 1997 by a group of young community members, aged between nine and fourteen, aided by one adult. The house is made entirely of chestnut and fir from the forest that belongs to the community.

The treehouse consists of a single room of 50 x 50 ft (16 x 16 m), plus three windows, a door, and a large balcony. The wooden supporting structure was constructed using ropes and nails; rope alone was used to attach the house to the tree. Stretching between the south side of the house and two other large trees is a cargo net – like a giant hammock – that's brilliant for jumping on or even sleeping in. You can leap onto the net from the balcony of the treehouse.

The youngsters wanted to build the treehouse to use during the spring and summer – for playing, socializing and sleeping in. Being young people they were very keen to build the house all by themselves, and though they did request the help of an adult, most of the work was done by them alone. They still go to the house and maintain it, although a new group of youngsters now also uses it.

The Tentyris community plans to become an 'international village', and people from all over Europe – and beyond – have started to settle there. May the treehouse tradition flourish within the expanded community.

LEPRE VIOLA

CONCEIVED OF AND BUILT BY THE COMMUNITY'S YOUNG PEOPLE, THE TENTYRIS TREEHOUSE
IS A GREAT PLACE TO HANG OUT, PLAY, AND SLEEP OVER.

TREE TRIBE FORTRESS

Simon: My treehouse was at Fairmile tree protest camp near Ottery St Mary in Devon, south-west England, on the path of the proposed re-routing of the A30 road. We called ourselves the Quercus tribe, after the Latin name for oak. The main focus of our camp was a 400-year-old fully crowned oak tree, which housed some tree dwellings, but I lived at the top of a three-storey fortress in a beech tree.

Getting into my treehouse was tricky, but eventually it became second nature. I had to put on a harness and climb up the branches, through a trap-door into the first treehouse (Niki's), past the next, then higher still to mine at the top, 80 ft (24 m) up. It was a difficult climb in wind or rain, and not to be attempted when drunk!

My treehouse was made of cargo netting that was tied to very flexible top branches. A web of rope was woven over the top of the netting, and then a tarpaulin was slung over the web. Cheap blue plastic tarps were all we could afford. They're noisy and quite flimsy, and we lost a few to the winds.

I had another tarpaulin on the floor with a carpet on top, and as a result my house was quite cosy inside, a bit like a nest. At 10 × 3 ft (3 × 9 m) there was just room enough for me and the occasional visitor – though it had to be someone I knew quite intimately! I had loads of snuggly blankets and a metal box to keep the squirrels out of my personal food stash. The floor was unstable and it rocked when I stood on it – like standing on a trampoline when someone else is jumping on it.

Others on the camp had elaborate treehouses with double glazing, but I was happy in my little cocoon, feeling safe there, even though it was right at the top of the tree.

Anyone going home from the communal house could climb the beech and then take one of the multitude of walkways to their own treehouse. There were two ropes: one to walk on, and one on which to lock the harness. The overall effect was of a star-shaped web of robes spreading out from the beech tree hub.

The camp lasted just over two years, and I lived in my treehouse for eighteen months. I was there at the eviction in January 1997, and came out at the end of the second day. All the trees are gone now, and no trace of the camp remains.

INGRID CRAWFORD

"ORIGINALLY PEOPLE JUST PUT UP NETS AND PLATFORMS TO STOP THE TREES BEING CUT DOWN, BUT GRADUALLY THEY WERE TURNED INTO FULLY BLOWN TREEHOUSES."

OUTLAW HIDEAWAY

Paul Reed: My friend Scotty (real name William Scott Scurlock) used to live in a three-storey treehouse deep in the woods of Thurston County, Washington. He earned his living from occasional carpentry jobs, and later from a series of bank robberies around Seattle. A master strategist, he also earned the name 'Hollywood' because of his many disguises. What he did with the stolen money is not fully known.

I first knew Scotty when we were students at the progressive Evergreen State College, Olympia, around 1980. When I later returned to Olympia as a lawyer, I used to drop by at his treehouse occasionally, or bump into him at a downtown restaurant.

In October 1992 I contacted Scotty and asked to 'borrow' his treehouse for a romantic interlude. Sensing that the house would not last forever, I took photographs to preserve it in my memory. Sure enough, within five years Scotty was dead and his treehouse put up for sale. Police cornered Scotty on Thanksgiving Day 1996, after his final heist, and he died by his own hand.

Scotty and a friend, Mickey Morris, built the treehouse at the back of a densely wooded 20 acre (8 ha) property. Supported by stands of Douglas fir and cedar, it appeared to 'grow' up from the forest floor (indeed, its construction evolved, and the house kept growing, over more than a decade). Starting with a simple platform in the trees, they used donated wood (probably stolen lumber, too) and hand tools to create a structure that eventually became Scotty's permanent residence.

Scotty's building methods were erratic — a friend described them as 'cosmic carpentry'. Neglected once erected, some parts of his treehouse later became dilapidated and even

PAUL S. REED

"THIS WAS NO SIMPLE TREE CABIN BUT A MULTI-STOREY DWELLING WITH PLUMBING, WIRING, A SLEEPING LOFT AND A FIREMAN'S POLE FOR HASTY EXITS."

dangerous – including the long wooden walkway that was a kind of back garden and look-out area. While it lasted, however, this was Scotty's "stairway to heaven", a magical pathway extending hundreds of yards along cedar lanes, high above the forest floor. From a practical point of view it also meant that Scotty could see anyone approaching his treehouse well in advance. Few back gardens could compete with Scotty's – and fewer still would dare.

For those approaching, the view was equally dramatic – if perhaps not at first. On Scotty's semi-rural property, past his farmhouse known as the 'gray house', a driveway extended to a small renovated barn. (Here the police were later to find Scotty's make-up, disguises, weapons, and a number of secret hiding places.) Past the barn, the driveway became not much more than a dirt path that wound through some trees until it reached a meadow. Here a narrow path led further into the woods, which gradually became denser

and darker. Suddenly the shrubbery thinned out, the surrounding cedars loomed larger, and Scotty's treehouse stood straight ahead. Unless a visitor were looking for it, they wouldn't see it right away. Then they'd notice the staircase, glance upwards, and gasp at the sight of Scotty's den. Was it really the highest treehouse the world? Seen from below, it certainly seemed so.

This was no simple tree cabin with four walls and a roof, but a multifaceted, multi-storey dwelling of around 1,500 sq. ft (140 sq. m) with thirty windows, plumbing, wiring, a sleeping loft, a wood-burning stove and a fireman's pole for hasty exits, as well as small hidden areas – hideaways within the hideaway. The interior was well furnished, with a large sundeck extending outwards – "a landing pad for angels", said Scotty.

Like its creator, the Scurlock House was a singular product of its time, place and making – and will no doubt remain infamous for a long while to come.

PAUL S. REED

BEHIND SCOTTY'S TREEHOUSE A LONG WOODEN WALKWAY AMONG THE CEDARS PROVIDED
A BACK GARDEN AND A VANTAGE POINT FOR SPOTTING UNWANTED VISITORS.

SUNRISE AND SCULPTURES

Jürgen Bergmann: I have been a fan of treehouses ever since my childhood. When I was young I used to create all sorts of strange structures. Now I have my own company, the Künstlerische Holzgestaltung ('Creative Wood Sculptures Company'), based in eastern Germany. The company is dedicated to the creation of playful combinations of nature, art and culture. Our designs include everything from public sculptures to landscaped playgrounds – but treehouses are a recurring theme.

My own treehouse is a three-storey structure about 30 ft (9 m) up a two-hundred-year-old oak tree. It has developed naturally, in stages, over the past twenty years. Access is via a long and rather forbidding pole bridge. Each storey represents a different style of treehouse: there is a bird's-eye seat in the crown of the tree, a sheltered platform, and a walled-in living space.

The main room is an enclosed area with windows and a door. It has clay-plastered walls and a wood-burning stove, and is simply furnished with cupboards, a bed and a bench. I can live comfortably here. Generally I use this room when I have to concentrate on writing. I bring my laptop up here, and don't come down until I'm through.

The middle storey is an open-air roof space with seating all around. It's a perfect place to have a party. My favourite bench is on this level, with a view over the river Neisse and towards Poland. (As we are on Germany's eastern border, from here I am the first German resident to see the sun rise!)

A table and bench make up the top storey. Sitting here, hidden amongst the spindly topmost branches of the tree, I feel very close to the sky. It is the ideal place for me to conjure up new wood sculptures and treehouse projects.

JÜRGEN BERGMANN

HIGH UP IN AN OLD OAK TREE, A THREE-STOREY TREEHOUSE PROVIDES
THE PERFECT CREATIVE HIDEAWAY.

A SPHERE IN THE TREES

Ian Christoph: In 1973, my friend Matt Darriau and I decided to build a treehouse. I was in 9th grade and Matt in the year below. Matt's mother had just bought some undeveloped woodland near Bloomington, Indiana. There was no electricity, water, or roads.

We had read the *Dome Book* and *Dome Book 2* – spin-offs from the counter-culture bible the *Whole Earth Catalog* – which espoused the benefits of using geodesic geometries, as originally popularized by Buckminster Fuller. Of all shapes, the sphere has the greatest interior volume for a given amount of surface area. We decided to build a sphere suspended from three separate cables. The structure was to resemble a massive hanging flower pot in the trees.

We scrounged timbers from Matt's mother, who was building a cabin, and salvaged barn wood for the sidings. The steel support cables came from abandoned limestone quarries. The framework was made from standard pine beams of 2 × 4 in. (50 × 100 mm). Five or six of these radiated from each node, and were connected to each other by a commercial metal strapper.

We planned to make a hemisphere, with a foundation of two large 4 × 10 in. (100 × 250 mm) planks running through the middle. We built the skeleton on the ground, raised it using a boat winch combined with three ratcheting fence stretchers, and hoisted the hemisphere 35 ft (10.5 m) into the air and lashed the cables to the trees.

We added a lower level, an upper level that extended out to make a deck running half-way round the dome, and an upper roof. We spent many nights sleeping out in the treehouse, experiencing the strange sensation of rocking and swaying gently – sometimes not so gently – high up in the Indiana trees.

MATT DARRIAU

CHRISTOPH AND DARRIAU'S AMBITIOUS TREEHOUSE FOLLOWED THE PRINCIPLES OF THE GEODESIC DOME, A SYSTEM MADE FAMOUS BY THE ARCHITECT AND VISIONARY BUCKMINSTER FULLER.

KANGAROOS AND COBWEBS

Julius Bergh: We first visited The Boomerang Farm about fifteen years ago, and it became a great favourite with my family. Lying in the hinterland of Australia's Gold Coast, Queensland, it was a place where people made boomerangs and taught you how to throw them. Tame kangaroos wandered around the grounds, and there was also a reconstructed pioneer's home. The farm had a few famous students: the Beatles, Abba, and even some visiting British royals all had a go at throwing the boomerang here.

The timber and corrugated iron treehouse, built into in a fig tree at the side of a creek, was intended to be an 'adventure' for kids of all ages visiting the farm. Nobody ever lived in it, but it certainly captured the imagination. To add to the sense of adventure on the approach you first had to walk through a narrow, dark 'mine tunnel' built from huge rocks. Many a scream could be heard as people made their way through this dark passage. Spiders' webs would stick to your face, but they weren't poisonous – or were they?

When you got out of the mine shaft you had to brave a rope ladder leading to a suspension bridge that was just one plank wide. Only the brave were rewarded with entry into the treehouse – but what a reward it was. Being up there felt like walking into an old movie set. There was an iron bed frame from pioneering days and a battered zinc basin for washing up, and some of the walls were covered in newspapers dating from the 1920s. A ladder led up to a turret at the top.

The Boomerang Farm eventually went the way of many farms on the Gold Coast: it was turned into a golf course. The treehouse is still there, however – as are the kangaroos.

JULIUS BERGH

NOT FOR THE FAINTHEARTED: AFTER BRAVING A 'MINE TUNNEL', VISITORS TO THE BOOMERANG FARM TREEHOUSE HAD TO CROSS A NARROW ROPE SUSPENSION BRIDGE.

PUBLIC ART, PRIVATE BEDROOM

Mikael Genberg: I'd worked as an artist for several years, creating paintings, installations and sculptures. But by 1996 I was ready for something else – I longed to escape from the galleries, and nature was calling me outside.

My dream was to be able to occupy people with my art for at least a couple of hours, even a day or night. And so I set out to create a series of alternative dwelling-places that would be freely available to borrow. The first was a treehouse, begun in August 1997. With the permission of the landscape architect in my home town of Västerås, Sweden, I chose the largest oak in the biggest park in the town centre, and began to build.

I wanted to build in harmony with nature, so I didn't use any nails: the structure is suspended from wires some 42 ft (13 m) high. I built it on location in the tree, piece by piece. The biggest problem was how to secure a steady foundation. Luckily I'd found an oak that forked into four sturdy branches; this meant that the house could hang inside them and pull the tree inwards. When the wind is strong, the tree and the house sway together.

The treehouse has a single bedroom, a toilet and a kitchen, and is simply furnished with a table, chair and hammock. It also has a tabletop heater, a telescope, books, a couple of lanterns and, of course, a fire extinguisher.

By the time the house was nearing completion it had become clear to me that I couldn't loan and maintain the treehouse for nothing. That's why I created the concept of the Hotell Hackspett ('Woodpecker Hotel'), and so far I've had more than 250 satisfied guests. Few can imagine beforehand the beauty and strength of the experience of spending a night in a tree.

MIKAEL GENBERG

MORE THAN 250 GUESTS HAVE STAYED AT MIKAEL GENBERG'S WOODPECKER HOTEL.
THE ARTIST HELPS THEM UP (AND DOWN) WITH A ROPE HARNESS.

AN INFINITE INTERCONNECTEDNESS

Daniel Susott: This very special project is dedicated to the happiness of all beings. The Biosphere Tree is a great Indian banyan flourishing in the lush Manoa Valley on the Hawaiian island of Oahu. It is part of what I call my Gayasphere, a living dome of giant bamboo and lineage-holder bodhi trees (related to the tree under which the Buddha traditionally attained enlightenment) woven together with sacred and medicinal vines. Although the Gayasphere covers only half an acre (2,000 sq. m) of sloping land, I like to think that when you view it as a series of interconnected 'spheres within spheres', it becomes infinite.

Within the great banyan sits a seven-levelled 'treehouse' – a collage of floors suspended below transparent roofs. A central pyramid of giant bamboo pierces the canopy of the tree, allowing a sweeping bird's-eye view of the valley and the sea beyond Waikiki. A stream flows through the Biosphere Tree's many secondary trunks. The highest level, 120 ft (36 m) above the stream, is a holy place.

In terms of energy we aspire to become completely 'off the grid', yet with all the comforts of home. We use 12-volt electricity to light the tree, and solar panels are planned. On the lowest level is a bathroom complete with composting toilet. The tree's name is a kind of joke, referring to the Biosphere 2 'planet in a bottle' experiment in the Arizona desert.

Access to the treehouse is by a hanging bridge, which connects the sloping hillside to the heart of the tree. A steel star dome, 7 ft (2 m) in diameter, swings like a pendulum over a pool in the stream. Originally this was planned to be a "meditation station", but it's now just a fun ride.

DANIEL SUSOTT AND GREG SOCITO

"THE SEVEN-LEVELLED TREEHOUSE IS A COLLAGE OF FLOORS SUSPENDED BELOW TRANSPARENT ROOFS" – AND COMES COMPLETE WITH SWINGING STAR DOME.

The treehouse was begun thirty years ago by the property's former owner Bob Durant; I bought the place from him in 1984. The treehouse then was just a platform accessed by a hanging bridge; Bob had started it as a project for the neighborhood kids. The neighbors still visit and hang out, and those who helped to build it now come by with their own children. Since those early days the treehouse has grown with the tree – banyans grow up and out in all directions, sending down wispy aerial roots that connect to the earth to form strong ancillary trunks, or entwine with branches below to support the higher branches.

Near the top of the tree, at the newest and largest level, lives artist Richard Gee. He was responsible for hoisting the bamboo for the pyramid into the heart of the tree, and now oversees the ongoing Gayasphere building project. He uses pulleys and zip lines to bring building materials across into the tree; this avoids having to carry them down the slope and across the bridge. A current project is to put glass floors in several strategic places, so you can enjoy the view down over the forest and stream.

Blessed by Tibetan rinpoches, the Biosphere Tree is host to the Buddhist Peace Fellowship, whose monthly meetings begin with teaching and meditation in the tree. As many as sixty people have celebrated in the tree at one time. Full-Moon Sacred Sound circles occur here, and 'starving artists' participating in the Hawaii International Film Festival often take shelter in the treehouse. (Arthur C. Clarke, Quentin Tarantino and a host of other celebrities have found fun and relaxation here while in Hawaii – their autographs grace the big bamboo.)

Besides being a venue for cultural and spiritual events, the treehouse is a fun place to sleep; you are lulled into slumbers by the sounds of the wind, the rain and the stream, and awaken to the early morning 'bird symphony.'

DANIEL SUSOTT AND GREG SOCITO

"DEDICATED TO THE HAPPINESS OF ALL BEINGS", THE BIOSPHERE TREE IS A PLACE FOR
RELAXATION, MEDITATION, AND HAVING FUN.

PASSIONATE PROFESSIONALS

Helena Petre: John Harris, founder of Scotland-based treehouse designers and builders Pear Tree, is a man with a passion for all things arboreal. As a child he spent "thousands of hours" in a treehouse in his parents' garden — made from a pallet and some packing cases — and he later spent his honeymoon in a treehouse in Malaysia. Harris built his first treehouse for his children, and in 1997 created Pear Tree, 'builders of bespoke treehouses'. Since then the company has grown to include three full-time designers and eighteen builders, who between them create from four to six treehouses a week.

"A treehouse is a place of wonder and adventure", says Harris, "a place to get away from everyday stress, to relax, and to become one with nature." And although these structures evoke our childhood fantasies, Pear Tree's clients often have sophisticated requirements: "Almost half the treehouses we build are for adults to use. The men find treehouses adventurous, and the women find them romantic." Pear Tree projects encompass the whole treehouse spectrum from adventure dens to a hotel reception suite suitable for fifty guests. They are now even developing a range of treehouse accessories, to include cargo nets, bunk beds and swings.

Each structure results from a combination of the client's wishes and a sensitive response to the tree itself. "Every tree is different, so no two projects are exactly the same," says Harris. "We've learned from arborists how trees grow, and how to build with them, so that they can move along with the house we've built. Above all we want to keep a simple, rustic feeling, no matter how modern the facilities."

CAD IMAGE: GORDON BROWN

HIGH-TECH MEETS RUSTIC: A 3-D COMPUTER VISUALIZATION SHOWS THE
CLIENT HOW THE FINISHED TREEHOUSE WILL LOOK.

Much of the secret of Pear Tree's success lies in its meticulous design and workmanship. Every treehouse design is hand-drawn or planned using computer-aided design (CAD) systems, and building work is approached with great attention to detail. Pressure-treated timber is used to keep the structure's weight down, and polycarbonate is employed in place of the more hazardous glass. Galvanized steel bolts and brackets fix the timber to the 'heart wood' at the core of the tree trunk; nails are always avoided.

Wherever possible, rooms are round, built around the tree trunk, and limbs appear suddenly through roof and window spaces. Every branch is taken account of, and allowances are made for movement and growth — "they are designed to move as the tree sways in the breeze", says Harris. Neoprene collars around the limbs allow for maximum flexibility. Even with large, complex jobs requiring strong foundation timbers, Pear Tree takes great pains to ensure the treehouse is sympathetic with its arboreal host.

While most Pear Tree clients are based in the sunnier parts of southern England, the number of international projects is growing. A diverse client list includes a party of deerwatchers deep in the Gloucestershire forest; a retired professional who wanted a sanctuary in the sky in memory of a dearly-loved wife; and an erstwhile commuter who requested an office in an oak tree — reducing a journey time from two hours to one minute (with the bonus of magnificent views).

Pear Tree will often be asked to build a house for children, but with a platform for adults to use after hours as a drinks deck (nothing beats watching the sun set while sipping gin and tonic in a tree). Harris sees this as part of a trend towards treehouses as multi-purpose structures that span the generations. What better way could there be of keeping the passionate world of the treehouse alive and kicking?

LEANNE CAIRNS

AN OFFICE WITH MODERN FACILITIES AND THE ADDED BONUS OF A BASKET LIFT
TO RAISE DRINKS FOR AN EVENING REFRESHMENT.

AT HOME IN THE REDWOODS

Corbin Dunn: When I was young I used to conjure up elaborate plans to build treehouses. In high school my friend Chris and I built a platform in some Californian redwoods, and added walls and a roof to create a little play shack. It wasn't elaborate, but it did make me catch the treehouse bug.

This first treehouse, in Corralitos, California, became rather dilapidated because we didn't build it to last. Two years ago I decided to build a new one on top of the old. I wanted it to be simple, and to be built free-form so that I could improvise as needed during construction. The basic idea was to create a platform in the trees and then build a house on top.

One of the prime factors in any treehouse, as far as I'm concerned, is that it should be at one with its surroundings. For me this meant two things: lots of windows, and a deck. The deck allows me to visit nature outside, but also serves a utilitarian purpose: it's the perfect spot to hide a water heater!

Having lived in my treehouse for ten months, I find that the exterior and interior give visitors two very distinct impressions. At first, as you approach from the driveway, you get a glimpse of something indistinct in the trees — the massive redwoods truly dwarf the house. Then you notice the stairs and entrance and start to get that 'treehouse feeling', re-entering childhood memories: it speaks of a different time.

Once inside, however, people realize that my house isn't simply nostalgic. This is a space for living in, with a loft area for my bed, a little kitchen, and a bathroom. Viewed from afar, the treehouse brings out the child in you, but when you step inside, you're home.

CORBIN DUNN

"THE A-FRAME ROOF WAS AN IRONIC TOUCH. LITTLE CHILDREN DRAW PICTURES OF HOUSES WITH A-FRAME ROOFS, AND I WANTED TO RECREATE THAT 'HOUSE' FEEL HIGH UP IN THE AIR."

BUILDING A TREEHOUSE

A treehouse is a place where you can give free rein to your individual creativity, as the examples in this book show. But while there may be almost as many types of treehouse as there are types of tree, some general principles do apply. This section gives guidelines for siting, designing and building your own treehouse. But if in the end it all looks too daunting you can always call in a specialist treehouse company to help (see Resources).

Before starting out, check with local planning authorities whether there are any restrictions to building a treehouse. In some places, if a structure is below a certain size and not used as a permanent dwelling it will not need planning approval, but there may be restrictions on height or on windows overlooking adjacent properties. Safety is vital during construction so always use a safety harness, and tie this and any ladders firmly to a strong branch. Think before you act, and keep a first aid kit handy. And, most importantly, have fun!

Choosing the right tree from the two basic forms is the first step to building a successful treehouse.

Branching tree:
mostly deciduous

Straight and tall tree:
mostly coniferous

FIRST STEPS

First of all you need to choose your tree, and decide on a position within it for your treehouse. Think about what you want from your treehouse: will it be an adult hideaway or a kids' play area? If you are considering a treehouse for children keep it close to the ground: 5 ft (1.5 m) is fine, and seems much higher when you are up there. Consider whether you want your treehouse to be hidden or visible, and make sure it will not disturb other people.

Choose a mature, healthy tree and check that there are no special protection orders on it that may affect pruning. When selecting a tree it is best to consult a qualified arborist and if any pruning is necessary have this done professionally. Think about how you wish to access your treehouse (see p. 88) and what materials you are going to use (see p. 89). Whatever you decide, it's best to start small and simple.

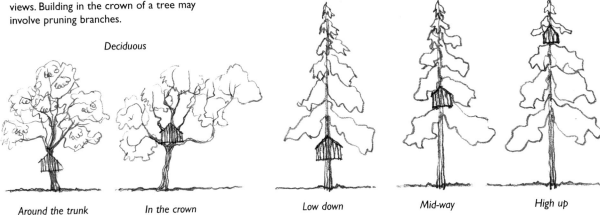

Consider your needs – low treehouses are easier to access but high treehouses give great views. Building in the crown of a tree may involve pruning branches.

Deciduous

Coniferous

Around the trunk   *In the crown*   *Low down*   *Mid-way*   *High up*

PLANNING PRINCIPLES

Every tree is different, so let the tree be your guide: follow the form of the tree, allow for growth and movement, and keep the structure lightweight. The position of the sun is another consideration to take into account. If you don't have one tree that seems right then several closely-spaced smaller trees will suffice; these may be supplemented with one or more posts sunk in the ground. Although some treehouse builders advocate a 'free form' approach, it's safest to plan the structure on paper before starting work. (For more on drawing plans see p. 90.) Allow for a deck if you want one, and don't make the treehouse too big for the size of the tree.

Treehouse sites can involve more than one tree, or a combination of tree and posts.

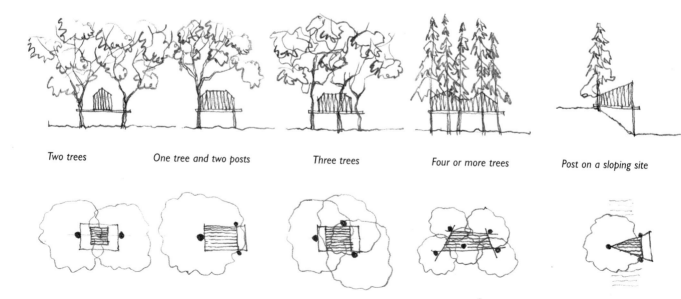

Two trees   One tree and two posts   Three trees   Four or more trees   Post on a sloping site

BUILDING A PLATFORM

The platform is the key element of almost any treehouse, providing a secure foundation for the rest of the structure. It should be built close to the trunk, with diagonal bracing for extra strength if it is not supported by branches or posts. Make sure the platform is level, and keep it balanced centrally around the tree to support uneven loads and reduce swaying. When securing the structure do everything you can to limit damage to the tree: rope lashing is preferable to nails, but make sure you know the right knots. Otherwise, choose strong galvanized or stainless steel coach (lag) screws, as ungalvanized nails will rust and encourage disease and rot. Don't cut the bark all the way round or constrict it too tightly with rope or wire – this can kill the tree.

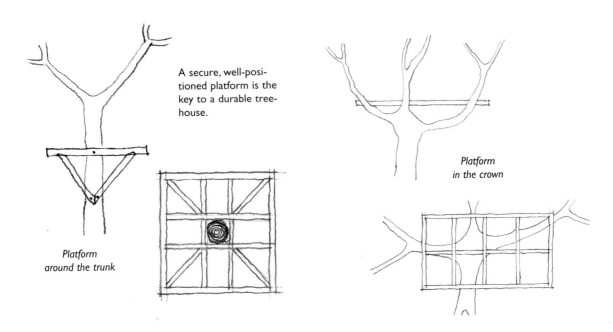

A secure, well-positioned platform is the key to a durable treehouse.

Platform around the trunk

Platform in the crown

FLOORS AND ROOFS

Once the platform is secure you then need to add the floor: for this you might use exterior plywood sheets or proper tongue-and-groove floorboards. The walls can either be built *in situ* up in the tree or prefabricated on the ground and then hoisted up into position — for larger treehouses the latter is much easier and safer. To minimize the amount of work done perched up in the tree you can even add external wall finishes on the ground (some options are shown on the opposite page), and pre-fix doors and windows. The roof may also be pre-assembled, but if branches are to penetrate it, or if it is an irregular shape, it is generally best to build it *in situ*. Once in position the roof can be covered with external plywood and finished with roofing felt (tar paper); or you can use battens and then finish with local materials such as recycled shingles, thatch or palm leaves.

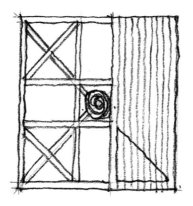

Tongue-and-groove boards provide an excellent floor for a sturdy platform.

Floor construction viewed from above

Step-by-step treehouse assembly

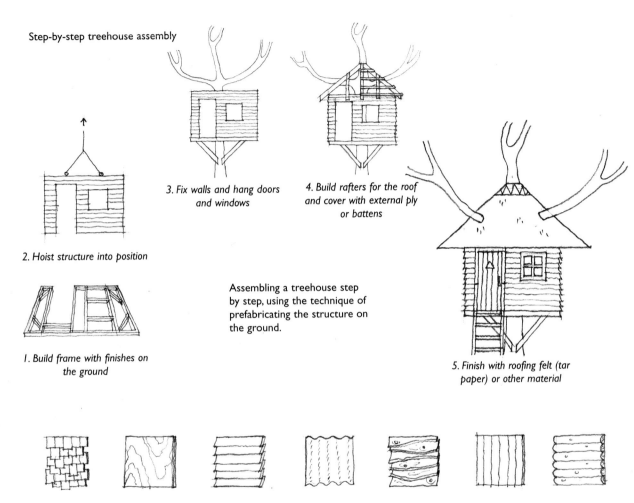

3. Fix walls and hang doors
and windows

4. Build rafters for the roof
and cover with external ply
or battens

2. Hoist structure into position

Assembling a treehouse step
by step, using the technique of
prefabricating the structure on
the ground.

1. Build frame with finishes on
the ground

5. Finish with roofing felt (tar
paper) or other material

Lightweight finishes: from left to right,
recycled shingles, external ply, overlapping boards, corrugated iron, rustic boards, vertical boards/siding, half-sawn poles

Medieval window

Top-hung shutter

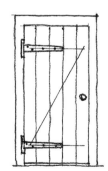

Skylight

WINDOWS AND DOORS

There's no need to adhere to convention in a treehouse – this is a place to experiment and to indulge your design fantasies. Whether your taste leans towards Gothic towers or rustic cottages, the possibilities for windows and doors are endless – the only important thing is to keep them in proportion to the size and design of the treehouse. For safety and lightness, use perspex or plexiglas instead of glass for windows. Try to use old or recycled items whenever possible (see Materials, p. 89).

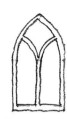

Gothic window

Porthole

Hexagonal window

Double casement window

Single-hinged window

Rising sun window

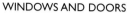

French shutters

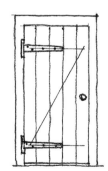

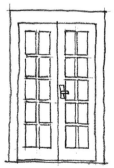

Ledged and braced door   *Farm/Dutch door*

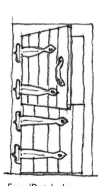

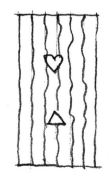

Double door

Wooden door with spy holes   *Trap door*

DECKS AND RAILINGS

Nothing can beat the experience of sitting outside a treehouse, right among the leaves and branches, on an outside deck, balcony or verandah. A deck can be part of the treehouse platform (it could be an extension constructed at a later date) or it might be in a separate place nearby, perhaps at a different level and reached by a rope bridge or wooden walkway. Whichever you choose, for obvious reasons the deck needs to be surrounded by safe railings. Functional these may be, but – as with doors and windows – you can still give your imagination free rein: some styles are shown below. For something different, why not make a giant hammock by attaching to the deck a strong rope net; spread with pillows and cushions it makes a great place to relax (see The Tentyris Community treehouse, p. 54).

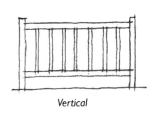

Vertical

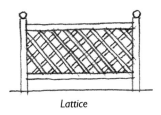

Lattice

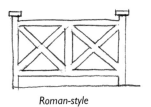

Roman-style

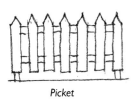

Picket

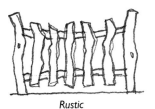

Rustic

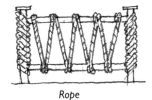

Rope

TREEHOUSE ACCESS

So much for building the treehouse – but how are you going to get up there? A simple wooden or rope ladder is fine if the house is not far from the ground, but steps (with handrails) are better for higher treehouses; spiral steps winding around the trunk are always fun and look more natural than a straight flight. If higher still, it is a good idea to break the journey with a series of landings, maybe with a small bench for rest stops. Sometimes it is possible to build a bridge or rope walkway from an adjacent tree, building or area of high ground. For really high treehouses a rope pulley system with a harness or chair may be the most convenient method – but you need to be prepared to abseil down. In fact, a rope pulley with a basket is indispensable for hoisting up provisions whether your treehouse is high or low.

Rope bridge

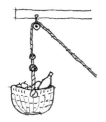

Pulley and basket

MAINTENANCE AND REPAIRS

After all the effort involved in designing and building a treehouse, the last thing you want is for it to fall down – especially if you happen to be inside at the time. Remember to check the floors, decks and railings frequently for rot or weakness; also inspect any steps, ladders and walkways, and repair any damage immediately. Check the tree annually for growth and movement, and adjust or refix attachments to the tree as necessary.

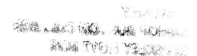

MATERIALS, FIXTURES AND FITTINGS

An eco-friendly treehouse means using as much recycled and waste material as possible. Building material suppliers and building sites are a good source of waste wood, ply and slightly damaged materials – but for structural use avoid wood with too many knots. Pressure-treated wood will last longer but may contain toxic chemicals, so wear gloves and don't breathe in sawdust. Avoid endangered tropical hardwoods at all costs, and only use new wood that is certified as supplied from sustainable managed resources. To avoid further depletion of Western Red Cedar, use only recycled shingles or shakes. Building reclamation depots are also wonderful places to find cheap supplies of old doors, windows, ladders, stoves and other interesting bits and pieces; salvaged materials help to give an individual touch, too.

To preserve and decorate your treehouse use non-toxic, eco-friendly stains, varnish and paints. If you plan to occupy your treehouse in relative comfort throughout the year you will need to insulate the floor, walls and roof, draughtproof the doors and windows, and preferably double-glaze the windows, too, so as to conserve energy.

If you plan to use electricity, rather than use the conventional supply go 'off grid' with photovoltaic panels and a wind generator (be careful to position these sensitively). You can then use low-voltage lights and equipment. For heating, nothing beats a real wood or coal fire but, to avoid the risk of setting the treehouse on fire, great care must be taken when siting the stove and chimney. For washing you can collect and recycle rainwater and heat it with solar power; but do not drink recycled water without proper treatment. A water-free or 'compost' toilet is an ideal eco-friendly addition, too.

MAKING PLANS

A simple sketch on graph paper is often sufficient to visualize your basic design, plot out measurements and check that you have allowed room for everything. Alternatively, there are many easy-to-use computer software packages that will allow you to draw plans, calculate dimensions and make adjustments to the design of your treehouse.

Karen and Frank Grayczk's treehouse

Corbin Dunn's treehouse

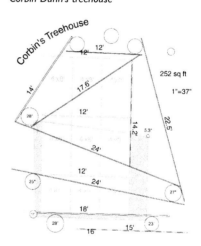

This sketch elevation and plan was produced by Karen and Frank Grayczk for their treehouse in Oregon (see p. 30).

This computer-generated plan of Corbin Dunn's treehouse (see p. 78) shows the position of the trees, main platform beams, and walls.

PROFESSIONAL SERVICES

If you choose to use the services of a specialist professional treehouse company, rather than building the treehouse yourself, you can expect more detailed plans. As well as drawing up ground plans and elevations, many companies can provide computer-aided three-dimensional drawings to show the completed treehouse in lifelike detail; an example from treehouse designers and builders Pear Tree is shown on page 75.

This plan and elevation was created by Leanne Cairns for Pear Tree, Scotland (see p. 74).

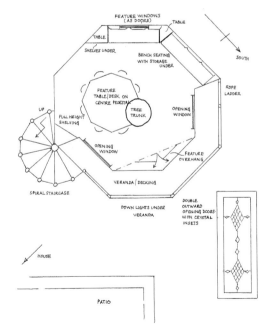

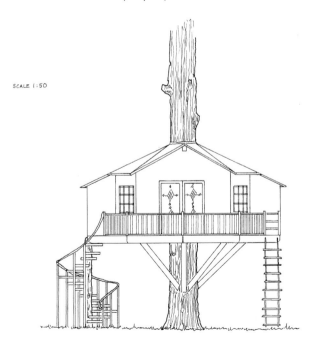

RESOURCES

BUSINESS

Biosphere treehouse, Hawaii
Owner: Daniel Susott
E-mail: info@treehousehawaii.com
www.treehousehawaii.com

Hotell Hackspett, Sweden
Owner: Mikael Genberg
Nygatan 4A, 722 14 Vasteras, Sweden
Tel/Fax: (00 46) (0) 4621830023
Mobile: (00 46) 7077 55393
E-mail: genberg@beta.telenordia.se

Bamboo Hooch, Puerto Rico
Owner: Jo Scheer
459 Normal Avenue, Ashland, OR 97520
Phone: (00 1) 541 482 6357
E-mail: bamboo@ADNinternet.com
http://netdial.caribe.net/~bamboo/index.h
tml reen

Green Magic Nature Resort, Kerala
Tourindia, Post Box #163, Mahatma
Gandhi Road, Trivandrum – 695 001
Kerala, South India
Tel: (00 91) 471 331507
Fax: (00 91) 471 331407
E-mail: tourindia@richsoft.com
www.richsoft.com/tourindia/

Out 'n' About Treesort & Treehouse
Institute, 300 Page Creek Road
Cave Junction, OR 97523, USA
Tel: (001) 541 5922208
or (in USA): 800 200 5484
E-mail: treesort@treehouses.com
www.treehouses.com

Treehouses of Hana, Maui, Hawaii
(and locations in Asia)
Owner: David Greenberg
E-mail: hanatreehouse@yahoo.com
www.maui.net/~hanalani/

Canyon Perch, California
Barbara Butler Artist-Builder Inc.
325 South Maple Avenue #37
South San Francisco, CA 94080, USA
Tel: (00 1) 415 864 6840
E-mail: barbara@barbarabutler.com
http://barbarabutler.com

Kunstlerische Holzgestaltung
Kulturinsel Einsiedel, Germany
Director: Jurgen Bergmann
02829 Zentendorf, Germany
Tel / Fax (00 49) (0) 35891 4910
E-mail: pop@kulturinsel.de
www.kulturinsel.de

Pear Tree, Scotland
The Stables, Viewfield, Fenwick, Ayrshire
KA3 6AN Scotland
Tel: (00 44) (0) 1560 600111
Fax: (00 44) (0) 01560 600110
E-mail: info@peartreehouse.com
www.peartreehouse.com

Treehouse Workshop, Llc
303 N. W. 43rd, Seattle, WA 98107
Tel: (001)206 784 2112
Fax: (001) 206 784 1424
E-mail: jake@treehouseworkshop.com
www.treehouseworkshop.com

Boomerang Farm, Australia
Mugeraba-Springbrook Road
Gold Coast, Queensland, Australia
Tel: (00 61) (0) 7 55305231

The Elms, New South Wales
Blackheath Real Estate
8 Govetts Leap Rd, Blackheath
NSW 2785, Australia
Tel: (00 61) (0) 2 4787 8231

John Gathright/John-san
TreeClimbingWorld, TreeClimbingJapan,
TreeHab
E-mail: johnsan@ruby.ocn.ne.jp
www.treeclimbing japan.com
www.johnsan.com

COMMUNITY

Damanhur Federation
10080 Baldissero Canavese, Italy
Tel: (00 39) 0124 512226
E-mail: tentyris@damanhur.org
www.damanhur.org

PROTEST

Beech Tree, Devon, England, no longer
exists. See Kate Evans' book (see p. 93)

Professional photographs of tree protest
sites and other "alternative" accommodation are available from:
Ingrid Crawford, Glastonbury, England
Tel: (00 44) (0)1458 835046

Mariah's Manor, California
Occupied by: Nate Madsen
www.upatree.net/main.html

PRIVATE OWNERS

Corbin's Treehouse, California
Owner: Corbin Dunn
http://gate.cruzio.com/~seaweb/corbin/tre
ehouse.html

The Edwards Treehouse, Georgia
Owner: Sam Edwards
www.samstreehouse.com

Treesnakes, Minnesota
Owners: Hazel and Filbert Treesnakes
E-mail: treesnakes@treesnakes.com
www.treesnakes.com

OLD-TIMERS

Geodesic Sphere Treehouse, Indiana
Created by: Ian Christoph and Matt
Darriau. Pulled down by the landowner.

Scurlock Treehouse, Washington
Created by: William Scott Scurlock and
Mickey Morris. Put up for sale. Refer to
Anne Rule's book (see right).
http://law.about.com/newsissues/law/librar
y/blscotty.htm

OTHER WEBSITES WE LIKED:

Fascinating links to many treehouse sites
can be found at:
http://gate.cruzio.com/~seaweb/corbin/tre
ehouse_links.html

Construction tips and world treehouses:
www.btinternet.com/~fulton/treehous.htm

Smithsonian magazine article on building
a treehouse:

www.smithsonianmag.si.edu/smithsonian/i
ssues97/aug97/treehouses.html

Do or Die online magazine, treehouses
and protest issues: www.eco-
action.org/dod/no7/38-39.html

Possibly the most famous tree protest in
the world, carried out by Julia Butterfly
Hill: www.lunatree.org/

Guest houses:
http://cedarcreektreehouse.com/
www.waipio.com/

Custom-designed and built treehouses
and playhouses:
www.peak.org/~sfales/treehouse1.htm

A tale of a child's backyard playhouse,
handbuilt by his father:
http://mckoss.com/platformhouse/

One man's dream: a chocolate factory
and a tropical bamboo treehouse:
http://grenadachocolate.com/bam-
boohouse_on_trees/

FURTHER READING

Aikman, Anthony *Treehouses* Robert Hale
Ltd, London, 1988

Bouchardon, Patrice *The Healing Energy of
Trees* Journey Editions, Boston and Tokyo,
and Gaia Books Ltd, London 1999

Evans, Kate *Copse: The Cartoon Book of
Tree Protesting* Orange Dog Productions,
Biddestone, Wiltshire. 1998

Merrick *Battle for the Trees* Godhaven Ink,
Leeds 1998

Nelson, Peter and Judy with David Larkin
The Treehouse Book Universe Publishing,
New York, 2000

Nelson, Peter and Gerry Hadden *Home
Tree Home* Penguin Books, New York,
1997

Nelson, Peter *Treehouses: The Art and Craft
Out on a Limb* Houghton Mifflin
Company, New York, 1994

Pearson, David *The Gaia Natural House
Book* Gaia Books Ltd, London, 2000

Pearson, David *The New Natural House
Book* Fireside, Simon & Schuster, New
York; Conran Octopus, London, and
Harper Collins, Australia, 1998

Pearson, David *The Natural House Catalog*
Fireside, Simon & Schuster. New York,
1996

Pearson, David *Earth to Spirit: In Search of
Natural Architecture* Chronicle Books, San
Francisco; Gaia Books Ltd, London, and
Harper Collins, Australia, 1994

Rule, Anne *The End of the Dream: The
Golden Boy Who Never Grew Up* Simon &
Schuster, New York, and Warner Books,
London 1999

Stiles, David and Jeanie *Treehouses you
can actually build* Houghton Mifflin
Company, New York, 1998

I N D E X

**Bold page numbers indicate
treehouse photographs**

A B

Alternative Energy Engineering 26
aluminum 20
bamboo 14, 42, 70, 72
Bamboo Hooch 13, 14-17, **15**, **17**
banyan 70, 72
barrels 36
batt insulation 46
beech tree 56
Biosphere Tree 70-73, **71**, **73**
boards 85
bodhi tree 70
Boomerang Farm 66-67, **67**
branching tree 80
bridge 28
Buckminster Fuller, Richard 64
Butterfly Hill, Julia 26

C D

canvas 49
Canyon Perch 28-29, **29**
cargo netting 54, 56
Cavaltree Fort 48
cedar 58
chestnut 54
children 28, 81
composition roll roofing 46
computer-aided designs (CAD) 76
coniferous trees 81
cooking 27
Corbin's Treehouse 78-79, **79**, 90
corrugated iron 22, 66, 85
Creative Wood Sculptures Company 62
Damanhur 54
deciduous trees 81
deck 24, 46, 87
diagonal bracing 83

doors 86
double casement window 86
Douglas fir 48

E F G

electricity 70
elevator 32
Elms, The 22-23, **23**
Engel Treehouse 44-47, **45**, **47**
entrance 26
exterior siding 20
Fairmile Protest Camp 56-57, **57**
fiberglass 26
fir 54
floors/flooring 16, 84
foundation 30, 68
four or more trees 82
French shutters 86
galvanized nails 83
galvanized steel bolts 76
Gayasphere 70, 72
Geodesic Dome 64-65, **65**
gothic window 86
Green Magic Nature
    Resort 13, 32-35, **33**, **35**
guava wood 42

H I J

handrails 46
heating 89
hexagonal window 86
hip roof 16
Hotell Hackspett see Woodpecker Hotel
hurricane resistance 16
insulation 89
Jungle Treehouse 40-43, **41**, **43**

K L

kerosene lamps 34
Künstlerische Holzgestaltung see
    Creative Wood Sculptures
    Company
ladder 44, 46, 66 see also Staircase
lattice railings 87
lighting 34

M N

maple trees 18, 30
Mariah's Manor 24-27, **25**, **27**
materials, sources of 89
medieval window 86
Miso Barrel Treehouse 36-39, **37**, **39**
nails 54, 83
Nelson, Peter 10
neoprene collars 76

O P

oak tree 18, 44, 56, 62
one tree and two posts 82
Out 'n' About Resort 48-49, **49**
Oxbow Annex 30-31, **31**, 90
Pear Tree 10, 74-77, **75**, **77**, 91
perspex/plexiglass 86
photovoltaic collectors 16
planning approval 80
planning principles 82
plastic 26
    roofing 20
platform 24, 83
playhouse 28
plywood 18, 46, 47
polycarbonate 76
post on a sleeping site 82
pressure-treated timber 76
pulleys 72
pulley and basket 88

Q R

railings 30, 47, 87
    Roman-style 87
raw materials 16, 48
recycled materials 36, 46, 50, 84, 85, 89
resources 92
roofs 16,18, 22, 26, 30, 84, 85
roof space 62
rope 26, 54, 56, 66, 87, 88

S T

safety 80
Samstreehosue 50-53, **51**, **53**
Scurlock House 58-61, **59**, **61**
seat 62
shed 20
skylight 16, 38, 86
solar panels 24, 70
solar power 24, 34
staircase/stairway 22, 42, 46
Swiss Family Complex 48
Tentyris Comminity 54-55, **55**
Three-in-one Treehouse 62-63, **63**
three trees treehouse 82
toilets 89
Treehouse Workshop 10
treehouses *see* Make It 80-91
Treesnakes 18-21, **19**, **21**
two trees treehouse 82

W

walkways 57, 60, **61**, 66
walls 26, 62, 84
water collection system 26
windows 20, 30, 50, 86
wires 68
Woodpecker Hotel 13, 68- 69, **69**

ACKNOWLEDGMENTS

Gaia Books is deeply indebted to each and every contributor to the treehouse stories in this book. Gaia Books would also like to thank the many people who have helped with treehouse research, mainly behind the scenes and for no personal gain:
ADSPR, Babu Varghese, Bill Compher, Barney Duly, Carol Venolia, Chip Baker, Chris Cocchi, Christian Gotsch, Elaine Rocheleau, Elspeth MacDonald, Frank Chambers, Gaia International, GEN-Europe, Gerardine Munroe, Godhaven Ink Publishers, Greg Van Mechelen, Hainault Park, Iliona Outram, Ingrid Crawford, J. Benecki, Jess Fuller, Jesse Troxler, John Juzdowski Jnr., Julia Butterfly Hill, Konstantin Kirsch, Laura Hartman, Linda Beech, Marcel Kalberer, Mark Laurence, Mona, Mott, Patrick Demers, Peter Harper, Roderick James, Roger Webster, Steve Hurrell, Suzanne Butler, Sybil Edwards, Sylvia Pearson, Sydney Baggs, Teena Albert, Theo Cocchi, Yozo Hirano.

David Pearson would like to thank the Gaia Team: especially Helena Petre for her indefatigable research work in searching out treehouse people around the world and compiling their fascinating stories; Sara Mathews and Thomas Hawes for their imaginative design; Christine Davis for her professional editorial work; Pip Morgan and Patrick Nugent for project management; and Charlie Ryrie for her early work. Last but not least, I would also like to thank everyone at Chelsea Green Publishing for their friendly and enthusiastic support.

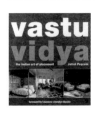